THOMAS
TALLIS

BY JESSICA SWALE

SERVING THEATRE

SINCE 1830

WWW.SAMUELFRENCH.CO.UK
WWW.SAMUELFRENCH.COM

FOR AMATEUR PRODUCTION ENQUIRIES
UNITED KINGDOM AND WORLD EXCLUDING NORTH AMERICA
plays@SamuelFrench-London.co.uk
020 7255 4302/01
UNITED STATES AND CANADA
info@SamuelFrench.com
1-866-598-8449
Each title is subject to availability from Samuel French, depending upon country of performance.

This text went to press during the rehearsal period and may differ slightly from what is presented on stage.

Thomas Tallis Programme Notes

'Music was my refuge. I could crawl into the space between the notes and turn my back to loneliness.'   Maya Angelou

Music has always been a source of solace, a means of transcending the everyday and escaping life's turbulence. And rarely has life in Britain been more turbulent than it was during the lifetime of Thomas Tallis. The composer, who lived under six Tudor monarchs, witnessed the country catapulting between religious factions, as monasteries burned and protestors were sent to their deaths. Rarely can there have been such a desire for eternal peace. And rarely has a composer succeeded in creating music quite as fittingly transcendent as Tallis.

Tallis' life is, for the most part, a mystery. Composers in his day were considered workmen, not artists; they enjoyed none of the celebrity of Beethoven and his contemporaries, they were simply craftsmen, like wheelwrights or farriers. Consequentially the details of their lives were never recorded. What lives on, of course, is their music, and that is where I began when I embarked on this journey.

Whilst writing about a man of whom we know so little might seem like a conundrum, it is precisely that mystery that appealed to me. Writers like the gaps in history; they allow us both to delve deeper and to invent. We like to curl up in libraries, sifting through old manuscripts for glimmers of character or conversation, and then assemble our pickings magpie-like and filling in the gaps ourselves. And there is no shortage of delicious first hand accounts of Tudor life. In the gruesome *Foxe's Book of Martyrs* I came across Mrs Prest, an outspoken protestant who left her idol-worshipping family to cause destruction in Catholic churches, before Mary had her burnt to death. Then, in recordings of Dr Dee's 'Conversations with Angels', encounters reveal the power of the occult in the Elizabethan Court. The question was not what to write, but what not to write. And the result is not so much a story as a tapestry, a piece which weaves together imagined scenarios and real encounters in an attempt to capture the flavour of life in Tallis' time, a little fact, a little fiction.

The play follows the parallel lives of Tallis and a priest from Waltham Abbey. Along the journey we wash up with an array of characters, from a lowly plasterer and Tallis' wife to the young Edward VII, each of whom felt the effects of political wheels turning beyond their control.

We begin in Henry's court, as the young King is squaring up to the Pope. Whilst Henry is competing with Rome and Wolsey for the best choir, in nearby Waltham, Thomas Tallis is composing for the Abbey. It wasn't long before Henry's feud with the Pope exploded, and Waltham Abbey fell victim to the dissolution, leaving its community reeling in its wake. Tallis, however, was lucky. He was to write for the King.

At Henry's death, the young Edward VII took the throne, and imposed Protestantism with revived strength. In addition to instituting the Book of Common Prayer and throwing Latin out of the church, Edward insisted that religious music had "too many notes." Ornate music, he believed, was the work of the devil and had no place in his new church. Tallis was forced to move away from beautiful polyphony and write to Edward's stringent demands for a simpler plainsong, a single word for a single note.

Later, when Edward died unexpectedly, Mary I reinstated Catholicism in the bloodiest possible way. Church music was again to be richer, Latin returned and Tallis was asked to write choral music to reflect majesty and glory.

In his final years Tallis wrote for Elizabeth I, who, though she outwardly returned the nation to Protestantism, kept a very different style of worship in her own private chapel, where she enjoyed all the grand decoration of ceremonial Catholicism. Music in her Chapel Royal must not only be ornate, she insisted, it must be glorious.

Tallis, who was most likely deeply Catholic himself, succeeded in bending his quill to the demands of each monarch. Unlike his student William Byrd, there is no evidence that Tallis protested against any of these impositions. One might ask whether, in being so willing to write to their will, he sacrifice his artistic and religious integrity, whilst others stood up for their beliefs. Yet, perhaps it was a position of strength. Perhaps he made it his mission to provide the people with sacred music, at all costs.

One might easily assume that being forced to write simple protestant tunes must have been a burden to a man capable of creating such complex polyphonic harmonies. But perhaps the challenge to write simply requires equal genius. What is remarkable is that his protestant tunes are as beautiful and often more haunting than the rich Catholic music he is best known for. I have found that it's often his simplest tunes which have haunted me as I've been writing. As da Vinci said, "Simplicity is the ultimate sophistication."

Thomas Tallis is the first new play written for the Sam Wanamaker Playhouse, and it has been a fascinating to discover how to tell a story in that space. It is completely unlike writing for the outdoor space. The open air stage is a gloriously blank canvas on which words are everything. There the actors can transform the space with a simple declaration welcoming us to the forest of Arden, tossing us on board a ship or transporting to the Holy lands. The outdoor space begs for bold characterisation, political landscapes, crowd scenes and statement.

In contrast, the Wanamaker is anything but blank; it exudes personality. Designed for Jacobean revenge tragedies, the candlelight, the smell of the wood, the gold, burnt umber and rich reds in the paint all transport us immediately into a dark and almost sacred space. In contrast to the public statement in the yard, inside performance feels so intimate they could almost be confidential. The audience are invited to listen to the minute cadences in every line. Here silence is powerful and, possibly most surprisingly, image becomes all important. It's akin to writing for film. Image is vital, and words are simply one aural tool, alongside music and silence. And unlike any other theatre space, here you can achieve a close up. A candle is like a camera; it guides our eye. A letter surreptitiously dropped on the floor will only be seen by the audience when the person discovering it shines their light upon it. Here a character can stand on stage and not be seen until he chooses to reveal himself. And like a close up, light defines tone and reveals thought. A malevolent plotter will light his own face, whilst two lovers, desperate to gaze at each other, will light the others' visages. And of course, like any good film, the effect of any image is amplified ten fold by music. We are so lucky to collaborate with The Sixteen on this piece. It is the perfect space for choral work and a wonderful backdrop for a play about religion. It has been a privilege to go on this journey and I do hope you enjoy it as much as I have.

Jessica Swale
October 2015

Thomas Tallis was originally performed in the Sam Wanamaker Playhouse at Shakespeare's Globe in 2014 with the following cast:

Brendan O'Hea   Thomas Tallis/Bishop/Guard

Susie Trayling   Elizabeth I/Queen Catherine/The Commisoner/
Joan/ Bethan/ Mrs Prest/Mary

Simon Harrison   Henry VIII/The Priest/The Pasterer/Mr Prest

Guy Amos   King Edward VI

Choir 'The Sixteen' featuring : **Kirsty Hopkins, Alexandra Kidgell,
William Purefoy, Jeremy Budd, Tom Raskin, Ben Davies**

Arngeir Hauksson   Lute

After a sell out run, it was revived in October 2015
with the following cast:

Brendan O'Hea   Thomas Tallis/Bishop/Guard

Katy Stephens   Elizabeth I/Queen Catherine/The Commissioner/Joan/
Bethan/Mrs Prest/Mary

Simon Harrison   Henry VIII/The Priest/The Pasterer/Mr Prest

Guy Amos   King Edward VI

The Sixteen : **Kirsty Hopkins, Alexandra Kidgell, William Purefoy, Jeremy
Budd, Tom Raskin, Ben Davies**

Arngeir Hauksson   Lute

Writer   **Jessica Swale**

Director   **Adele Thomas**

Designer   **Hannah Clark**

Creative Music Consultant   **Harry Christophers**

A NOTE ON THE MUSIC

Throughout the text there are music choices from Tallis' choral canon suggested for each scene. They are the songs we included in the original production, but they are not essential to performance. You could choose alternatives or cut the music as required.

Ideally, the play would be staged with a choir performing the music, but it could also be staged with recorded music.

Please note that although the music of Thomas Tallis is out of copyright, the arrangement is still in copyright, so please check permissions.

If you require information about the arrangements used in the original production please contact Samuel French.

Other work by Jessica Swale
published by Samuel French:

The Secret Garden
Sense and Sensibility
Far from the Madding Crowd

JESSICA SWALE

Jessica Swale is a writer and director. She is Artistic Director of Red Handed Theatre Company and a returning playwright at Shakespeare's Globe Theatre.

Plays include *Nell Gwynn* (winner of the Egerton Foundation New Play Award 2015), *All's Will that Ends Will* (Bremen Shakespeare Company) and adaptations of *Sense and Sensibility*, *Far from the Madding Crowd* (Watermill) and *The Secret Garden* (Grosvenor Park, Chester). Her first play *Blue Stockings* (Shakespeare's Globe) is now a GCSE set text. She is currently writing a new play, *The Mission*, about illegal adoptions in the 1920s. In 2012 she won a BAFTA JJ Screenwriting Bursary and has just completed an original screenplay, *Summerland*.

As director, credits include *Fallen Angels* (Salisbury Playhouse), *Bedlam* (Shakespeare's Globe); *The Belle's Stratagem* (Evening Standard Best Director 2012 nomination), *The Busy Body*, *The Rivals*, *Someone Who'll Watch Over Me* (Southwark Playhouse); *The School for Scandal* (Park Theatre); *Palace of the End* (Arcola), *Winter* (Theatre Newfoundland, Canada) and *Sleuth*, *Sense and Sensibility* and *Far from the Madding Crowd* (Watermill Theatre).

Jessica has also directed a number of Shakespeare plays in the Balkans and the Marshall Islands for the NGO Youth Bridge Global. She is author of a best-selling series of drama games books, published by Nick Hern. She trained at Central School of Speech and Drama and Exeter University.

For my Dad
To whom I owe my love of music
and a great deal more.

A PLAY IN ONE ACT

COMPANY

The play can be performed with four actors doubling, as below, or with a bigger company as desired. There are eighteen roles.

Actor 1 – **THOMAS TALLIS**, the **BISHOP**, **DR DEE**, the **GUARD**.

Actor 2 – **QUEEN CATHERINE**, the **COMMISSIONER**, **JOAN**, **BETHAN**, **MRS PREST**, **ELIZABETH I**, **MARY**.

Actor 3 – **HENRY VIII**, the **PRIEST**, **EDWARD**'s **ATTENDANT**, the **PLASTERER**, **MR PREST**.

Actor 4 – The Boy King *(***EDWARD***)*

The **GIRL** and the **SINGER** in Scene Two can be played by **SINGERS** or members of the company.

PROLOGUE

Thomas Alone

In the early years of **HENRY VIII**'s *reign.*

THOMAS TALLIS *walks onto stage. He holds a candle
and looks at the audience.*

THOMAS Listen.

Silence.

Listen.

He closes his eyes.

What do you hear? Silence.

He opens his eyes.

Silence – but for one sound.
This voice of mine. It lands so flat and dull.
And like a hammer, knocks upon the ear.
What voice is this to praise the Lord, my God?
What good is man with mortal voice of lead,
That treads flat foot across the realms of sound?
Where is the God in him? That voice is dead.
If this, my speech, so corpulent and cold,
Was all we had to say His name aloud,

Better no sound than that.

Better no sound.

Listen.

Silence.

Listen.

THOMAS *closes his eyes.*

A single voice sings an undecorated Amen. Then a more ornate Allelujah.

A sound divine.

A voice in song can flee the mortal man

And leave him shadowed lowly in his wake.

A note being sung will leave its host below.

And fly towards the gentle hands above.

So what think you of this – my simple thought.

That, if one boy in song may sound divine,

What if one son is coupled with his kin,

With son, and son, until they form a choir?

What better way have we to send our prayers

From churches, poor house, palace, monast'ry,

Where King in ermine bends his head in prayer

And pauper like him stoops upon his knee.

What better shape for worship can there be

Than song and choir to reach divinity?

We hear a choir sing (perhaps Videte Miraculum*). It is glorious.*

Scene One
The Italian Descant

In the early years of **HENRY VIII**'*s reign.*

A young (not yet rotund) **HENRY VIII** *is seated in his boudoir in night attire – a white billowing robe. A* **GIRL** *attentively rubs oil into his feet. A solo musician might play for his entertainment. The* **QUEEN** *(***CATHERINE** *of Aragon) enters.*

QUEEN How was the hunt?

HENRY I tired three horses. We coursed thirty miles before we caught the stag. He was magnificent. So much so I almost let him go.

QUEEN You are becoming soft, Henry.

The **QUEEN** *eyes the* **GIRL** *suspiciously.*

(dismissing the **GIRL***)* Leave us.

HENRY She does no harm.

The **QUEEN** *gives him a look.*

(to the **GIRL***)* Fetch me the boy from the chapel.

GIRL Sire. *(exits)*

HENRY *notices the* **QUEEN**'*s snide look.*

HENRY My boots were rubbing.

The **QUEEN** *kneels down and continues his foot massage. She's playing a game.*

QUEEN How's this? Better?

3

HENRY Somewhat.

She rubs harder.

Gently. I wish you'd seen the beast. So noble. He bent upon his knees before he died, like he was stooped in prayer – and looked at me.

QUEEN You sent for a boy. Who is he?

HENRY He's come from Rome. A castrato. They say he's touched by God.

QUEEN Who says?

HENRY Wolsey. The Pope was boasting that he had an Angel in his choir. So Wolsey sent to Italy, to fetch him for himself. So I have been sent to Hampton Court, to fetch him from Wolsey. His maze is better than mine, he cannot have a finer choir as well.

QUEEN Wolsey is ambitious. You should take him in hand.

HENRY *(on the massage – she rubs too hard)* Ow!

QUEEN He has an eye on Archbishop.

HENRY Are you interfering?

QUEEN No. Just… gently massaging.

HENRY Good.

*The **GIRL** comes back in with the **SINGER**.*

GIRL Sire.

HENRY Ah. The entertainment. Your reputation precedes you.

SINGER Your highness.

HENRY They say you are the finest Singer in Italy, is that right?

SINGER I believe so, Sire.

HENRY Well well. And in England? Who has the finest voice in my country? Do you think.

Is this a test? The **SINGER** *isn't sure.*

SINGER I...

You do, your Grace.

HENRY You speak the truth. But you may please me, before you return to Rome. Italy is the home of the sonnet. Dante. Petrarch. Tell me, do all your countrymen have such poetic souls?

SINGER Pardon me?

HENRY Lord knows mine don't. The English are far too busy spying on their neighbours and praying to idols to have time for poetry. What is it about Italy?

SINGER My Lord?

QUEEN Answer the King.

SINGER I cannot say. Perhaps it is the sun.

HENRY The sun?

SINGER We like to lie in the grasses. In the afternoons when it is too hot to work. Italians like to watch the sky. It is tradition.

HENRY Hm. You cannot lie in the grass in England. You get wet. Or bitten by an adder. Or mauled by peasants. Still, it's not all bad. We have a King. And no Pope. You sang in the Papal choir?

SINGER Yes, Sire.

HENRY How is the old bastard?

The **SINGER** *looks confused.*

Do you love him?

The **SINGER** *doesn't know what to say. He does love the Pope.*

Well? Do you?

A dangerous silence.

SINGER I…

No Sire.

HENRY Good. He is a traitor to God. Though we must thank him for parting with you; he must be very fond of you.

SINGER Yes.

HENRY I heard you were his favourite.

Dangerous pause. **HENRY** *thinks then pours a glass of wine.*

Well. Enough talk, you must sing for us, for what is life without music? Though first we must drink – to you.

HENRY *offers the* **SINGER** *a chalice of wine. The* **SINGER** *is reluctant, suspicious.*

Take it.

He takes it.

You will drink.

SINGER My Lord.

HENRY Go on. A toast. To Italy.

All eyes on the **SINGER**. *He raises the chalice to his lips and drinks the smallest sip.*

It is the very finest claret. Don't you like it?

The **SINGER** *drinks reluctantly. Is it poisoned? He waits a moment. Nothing happens.*

SINGER It is delicious.

HENRY Salute! And now, a song. What do you have for us?

SINGER A tune by Thomas Tallis, Sir.

HENRY Play on.

The **SINGER** *sings a* **TALLIS** *song (perhaps* Like a Doleful Dove*).*

Tallis, you say?

SINGER Yes, Sir.

HENRY Thomas Tallis. Is he an English man?

The **SINGER** *nods weakly. He is beginning to feel odd. The poison's done its work.*

You don't look well. Are you sick?

SINGER I...

The **SINGER** *dies.* **HENRY** *watches.* **CATHERINE** *looks on in horror.*

HENRY Take him away.

The **SINGER** *is taken out.* **HENRY** *and* **CATHERINE** *are left alone.* **CATHERINE** *is winded by watching the* **SINGER***'s demise, but she won't show it.*

What? *(pause)* Didn't you like the song? I found it rather charming.

CATHERINE My Lord.

HENRY I should eat. It's hours since I ate. Are you hungry?

CATHERINE No. *(pause)* No.

HENRY I shall dine. And then perhaps you might satisfy me.

*He leaves. She watches him go. Perhaps we hear music (***TALLIS***'E'en like the Hunted).*

Scene Two
The Dissolution

In the middle years of **HENRY VIII**'s *reign.*

We are at Waltham Abbey. Choral music plays (perhaps **TALLIS**' Videte Miraculum). *It is glorious, big, Catholic.* **THOMAS TALLIS** *is conducting the choir. A* **PRIEST** *is performing a Catholic ceremony in Latin. Incense. Crosses. Candelabras.*

Over the end of the music, a **ROYAL COMMISSIONER** (**COMM**) *arrives, a representative of* **HENRY**'s *court. He (or she) is collecting information for the Valor Ecclesiasticus, the summary of the church's property which* **HENRY** *is reclaiming for the crown. As the* **COMMISSIONER** *speaks, the* **PRIEST** *ceases his ceremony and listens. The music may well continue underneath.*

COMM One Abbey church and buildings on its grounds:

A nave, two pairs of transepts, Holy Rood,

One Lady Chapel, one small Eastern apse,

Cloisters, manor house and gate house too.

Four out-buildings, cellars, orchards, herb gardens and grazing fields. Farm land, 16 acres, from the Abbey to Waltham Holy Cross.

An annual income of one thousand and seventy-nine pounds, twelve shillings and one penny.

I hereby reclaim the buildings and all their contents under the orders of Henry the Eighth, by the Grace of God, King of England, France and Ireland, Defender of the Faith and of the Church of England.

8

PRIEST All of it?

COMM All buildings and their contents within. Listed here, the art works in the Abbey proper, golden crucifixes, statues, stations of the cross. Windows of stained glass, all pews and furniture, robes and fabrics, hymn books and Bibles in Latin, three hundred and eighty two in number, all to be removed or destroyed as the King sees fit.

PRIEST Please. They are our holy books.

COMM They are the Kings. *(holding up a bible)* And they are Latin. There is no place for Latin in the King's new church.

PRIEST It is the word of God.

COMM How can a beggar learn of God when all he hears are words in unknown tongue? These words are foreign – hollow. They're rhymed and jangled in every alehouse. There will be no more Latin. Not in prayer, nor in song.

THOMAS In song?

COMM No, indeed. From now on the Bible will be printed in English, read in English and sung in English. You ought to be delighted. They're far more likely to listen if they know what you are saying.

PRIEST And what of the Abbey? Does he intend to keep it?

COMM Perhaps. Or he might bestow it on some fellow who has pleased him. Or make it Protestant. Or burn it down.

PRIEST But it is a house of God!

COMM It is a pile of ordered stones. A building, sanctified by an Italian knave who claims to be divine, but has no more God in him than you do.

PRIEST What if we stayed without a fee? There's so much work to do here. The gardens run amock with goose grass. There's sowing and ploughing and if the cottages are not bound and thatched they will not last the winter. Please, we have no need of payment, we can live from the land, we do no harm. We ask for nothing but the right to stay.

COMM *(pause)* You have no right. You cannot stay.

PRIEST What would your King have us do then? Wander the lanes, beg for our supper? Dance for a coin?

THOMAS Father –

PRIEST What? *(to the COMMISSIONER)* What would he have us do?

COMM He is a generous man. You will be spared – provided you renounce the Pope and swear allegiance under oath. Then you will be free to retire, quietly. Out of sight. If I were you, I would disappear. *(to the PRIEST)* There's no place here for men like you.

PRIEST Holy men?

COMM Catholics.

PRIEST And if we will not swear?

COMM Then may the devil take your soul. You should pray he finds you first, as you will doubtless suffer less. Though you –

THOMAS Madam?

COMM You must wait to receive orders. The King has plans for you.

THOMAS For me? But he does not know me.

COMM The King has heard your songs, and, as good fortune would have it, he seems to like them. He has always been fond of a good tune. You are to write for him, for the new church and the Chapel Royal. I assume you will consent?

A pause.

Sir?

THOMAS *looks to the* **PRIEST** *and then back to the* **COMMISSIONER**.

THOMAS Of course.

COMM Excellent. Well, good day to you, God save the King.

THOMAS God save the King.

The **COMMISSIONER** *exits. The* **PRIEST** *can hardly look at* **TALLIS**. *Silence.*

Father –

PRIEST I have work to do.

THOMAS Let me help you –

PRIEST The night is closing in.

THOMAS *(moving towards him)* Peter, please –

PRIEST Don't touch me!

Silence. A stand off.

How can you even contemplate –

THOMAS What choice do I have?

PRIEST We all have a choice!

THOMAS It is my work! My calling.

PRIEST You are led by fear!

THOMAS *(a beat)* I won't write for the King, I write for God.

PRIEST He is a traitor to his God.

THOMAS Perhaps it is God's will.

PRIEST That's not the God I know.

THOMAS But what of Joan? If I condemn myself –

PRIEST What of the rest of us! I will not go.

THOMAS But you must!

PRIEST I will not renounce the Pope.

THOMAS Then he will have you killed!

PRIEST All I ask for is the chance to love the Lord. That is all! But he – he has overturned the world on a whim! For his lust. I will not swear to him, he has the devil in him.

THOMAS There are places. People will hide you.

PRIEST I do not wear my faith in shame.

THOMAS But your life!

PRIEST This is my life! The Lord is my shepherd.

THOMAS They know you are here. They will return. Let me help you.

> *Perhaps music plays (e.g.* O Nata Lux*).* **THOMAS** *takes the* **PRIEST**'s *hand in a moment of communion. The church is dismantled piece by piece, candles are snuffed out, until the stage is left bare, except a table.* **THOMAS** *sits trying to write in English. He tries singing a line.*

> *(sung)*
> GOD GRANT US GRACE.

> *Then as he writes, we hear it sung. He makes changes as he goes, scribbling, stopping, starting. He is struggling. English is not as beautiful as Latin. We listen to* Gaude Gloriosa.

Scene Three
A Single Word on a Single Line

When Young **EDWARD VI** *ascends the throne.*

As the song continues, **THOMAS TALLIS** *writes.*

His wife **JOAN** *arrives. She begins to carve a pear as she watches him work and eats the pieces from the knife. She takes a piece of manuscript and looks at it. She offers him a bite. He declines. He's writing.*

Then a **BOY KING**, **EDWARD VI** *arrives on the balcony, accompanied an* **ATTENDANT**. **TALLIS** *continues to write and tries to ignore the voices of the new King and the* **ATTENDANT** – *he can hear them but not see them.*

ATTENDANT The King is dead. Long live King Edward.

TALLIS *pauses. This is terrible news to him. He tries to write on.*

EDWARD This music. What is this? I hate it.

THOMAS *is shaken but writes on.*

There are too many notes.

EDWARD *holds up his hand. The music stops. Silence.*

JOAN Thomas?

He ignores her and tries to write. Nothing comes. She offers him some pear again.

Here, I just picked it. The sun's been kind. *(pause)* You have to eat something.

EDWARD The people are to hear the word of God. The word uncomplicated by vanity. The word in English. It is to be sung without ornament, without harmony; one note for every word. A single phrase on a single line.

JOAN Thomas, I can't live with a man of no words!

THOMAS A single phrase on a single line?

EDWARD I am the Supreme Head of the Church, the second Josiah and this Nation's most precious gem.

ATTENDANT Sire, you have a companion. A friend is here to play with you.

EDWARD I'm busy.

THOMAS My talent's turned to dust.

JOAN There was a time you thought you couldn't write in English.

THOMAS A single phrase on a single line?! That's not music. A boy in a playground could write that.

JOAN He is a boy.

THOMAS But he is King. And he is tearing at my soul.

EDWARD We will seek out the worms in the bud. The tyranny of the Bishops of Rome will be avenged and those who go against it will be damned. Here. *(handing a scroll to the* **ATTENDANT***)* Give it to the people. I have called it *The Pope as the Antichrist.*

ATTENDANT As you wish.

EDWARD And here are my stipulations for the composition of church music. Make them cease their infernal warbling. It is the word of God they sing – it does not require garnish.

ATTENDANT Of course, Sire. Shall I have your companions dismissed?

EDWARD You think I have an interest in conkers and skittles?

ATTENDANT Very well. Though your sister Elizabeth will join you for supper, if that pleases you.

EDWARD And Mary, she is to come too.

ATTENDANT Mary apologises. She has been invited to a masque. With the French.

EDWARD A masque?! With the FRENCH?! Absolutely not.

ATTENDANT Sire?

EDWARD She's not to go.

ATTENDANT But Sire –

EDWARD They mustn't see her dancing!

ATTENDANT Your grace, even your dear Father wouldn't have objected to a little *pas de deux*.

EDWARD My father was weak. Tell her she is no longer to attend these foreign merriments; it doesn't become a Christian princess. We are a serious nation, we do not dance!

ATTENDANT You can tell her yourself.

EDWARD What did you say?

ATTENDANT Nothing, Sire.

EDWARD Then don't speak, if you have nothing to say. *(pause)* Well?

ATTENDANT There is a small matter. Your companion Lord Seymour.

EDWARD Yes?

ATTENDANT He is accused of embezzling funds – from the royal purse. He asks that you, his once familiar friend, might pardon him.

EDWARD He taught me mathematics.

ATTENDANT Indeed.

EDWARD And gave me pocket money.

ATTENDANT He has been kind to you.

EDWARD And in Edinburgh, he put all to fire and sword at my command. He razed the town in a day. And taught the false Scots that God will avenge the disloyal.

ATTENDANT So you will give him your pardon?

EDWARD No. Send him to the gallows. He was sour to me last Tuesday.

ATTENDANT Your grace.

EDWARD Have those orders sent to every church.

ATTENDANT My Lord.

EDWARD And see they are enforced!

They exit.

THOMAS A single line of notes? A single line?!

I want to write music, Joan – and harmony! To make on Earth the sound of angels. To conjure heaven. How can I, with every note within my grasp, with every tone and chord and all polyphony, write something wondrous on a single line? With all the voices of the choir, each sacred interval, tone and triad, with every sound of God... silenced? It is sacrilege. Base. And leaves me a sunken nothing.

JOAN Every sound in nature is a single tune. The night jar in his nest. The owl his piping notes. That is God's song. Just listen, dear heart, and have patience. You will find your way. *(pause)* Father Peter has gone.

THOMAS Gone?

JOAN I went to take him bread, but the barn was empty.

THOMAS He may return. You thought he went before.

JOAN The blankets are gone. The flagon, and his bible.

THOMAS How long ago? We may reach him.

JOAN The straw was cold.

THOMAS He is not safe.

JOAN So we must pray for him. It is not for you to worry. You have too much in your heart already. Thomas, Edward will not wait.

They sit in silence. A nightingale sings.

THOMAS *begins composing. We hear a piece of music in which a single voice is joined by another and another until the whole choir are singing (for example* God Grant Us Grace*). The result is magnificent in its simplicity.*

Scene Four
The Peddler's Box

Several months later, during **EDWARD** *'s harsh reign.*

A **PEDDLER** *enters. He is the* **PRIEST** *from Waltham Abbey, now disguised. He has a box of wares, covered in horse skin. It is knocked about, as is he.*

PEDDLER *(sings or speak sings)*
FELLOWS, LADIES, WHO WILL BUY?
LET MY TRINKETS TAKE YOUR EYE,
WHAT WORTH IS A COIN, SAY I,
IF IT AIN'T SPENT AFORE YOU DIE?

HERE BE BALMS AND SALVES OF ROSES,
FINE DISGUISES FOR YOUR NOSES,
TINCTURES FOR YOUR SOUND REPOSES,
WARD OFF DEATH WITH HERBAL POSIES.

BUY THEM FROM THE PEDDLER – O,
'FORE HE ON HIS JOURNEY GOES
THOUGH WHERE HE'S GOING, NO MAN DOTH
    KNOW…
NO-ONE?

A local lady, **BETHAN,** *has entered.*

BETHAN What have you in your box, Peddler?

PEDDLER *(to himself)* My luck has turned.

(to **BETHAN***)* Whatever pleases you, my lady. You shall find it in my trunk, I guarantee it.

BETHAN You're very bold for a beggar.

PEDDLER All I have are my trinkets and my wit. So I shall try and please you. What is your heart's desire? I shall sell it to you.

BETHAN True love and life long happiness.

PEDDLER I've just run out of that. How about some soap?

BETHAN I have soap.

PEDDLER *(offering her a candle)* Or candles?

BETHAN I have candles.

PEDDLER *(offering her some lace)* Or lace?

BETHAN And lace.

PEDDLER Ah, but not Nottingham lace? It is the weave of the ancient loomers, I purchased it myself from my lady Acorn, who'd sit under the rafters crafting her weave by moonlight. Tuppence?

BETHAN You trade in fables too.

PEDDLER I trade in anything you'll pay a penny for.

BETHAN Let me see those beads.

PEDDLER *(taking them out)* You have a fine eye, Madam. These are strung on the silk of a mulberry worm. Plucked from his cocoon. It is the strongest silk you ever will see.

BETHAN And what are the beads?

PEDDLER They grew upon a bead tree. I picked them myself.

BETHAN *(looking in the box)* You're selling slate?

PEDDLER No. Not I.

BETHAN *(taking the slate out of the box)* Then what is this?

He is unsettled.

PEDDLER It is my adding slate. It's not for sale.

BETHAN A shame. You won't sell it – even for sixpence?

PEDDLER Madam. I have trinkets and fancies to tickle your cockles, look here, waxes and wools –

BETHAN *(holding up a chalice)* A chalice?

PEDDLER A bodkin, a peas cod –

BETHAN Eternal life?

The **PEDDLER** *stops in his tracks.*

PEDDLER *(pause)* Eternal life? No Madam.

BETHAN Father. *(pause)* Rosary beads? An altar stone?

PEDDLER I don't think I can help you.

BETHAN Pewter cups and candlesticks? They will hunt you out.

PEDDLER Madam –

BETHAN *Deus nobiscum –*

PEDDLER *Quis contra.*

She takes his hand and he lays his hand on hers.

Can we be seen?

BETHAN No. But we must not tarry. There are others in the Parish. We meet when we can, but we have no one to confess to, or to bless us. Would you say mass with us?

PEDDLER I need somewhere to sleep.

BETHAN To stay?

PEDDLER Do you have a barn? An outhouse.

BETHAN Father…

PEDDLER Anywhere.

BETHAN I have a family.

PEDDLER I need to sleep. Just for a short time.

BETHAN I have two young ones. If anyone found out.

The **PEDDLER** *lifts his sleeve to show a bruised, cut arm.*

PEDDLER They tried to steal my box. It is not safe. Please, I have walked through twelve nights straight.

BETHAN Father...

PEDDLER Have you a sty? Or a coop. I will sleep in the mud, just please... rest. And bread. And I will pray with you.

She takes a moment to think. Then she indicates for him to follow her. As they walk away, a man steps out of the darkness and watches them go.

Scene Five
Noses Out of Joint

Under Mary Queen of Scot's Anti-Protestant reign.

At Waltham Abbey, the **PLASTERER**, *sits making a paste. He is restoring the figures in a Catholic frieze in which the saints have been damaged.* **THOMAS TALLIS** *walks through with some books.*

PLASTERER If you're looking for the Priest, he is praying yonder. *(looking up)* Eh! Where are you going with them? You put 'em back.

THOMAS Good Sir, they are my own.

PLASTERER You sure you're not one of them divers? Swipers?

THOMAS No, I assure you. I worked here once and left these behind. I thought I'd have no need for Catholic tunes again.

PLASTERER You a musician?

THOMAS A composer, yes.

PLASTERER I watched it when they pulled the chancel down. It took two dozen men to move the stone. Sold it for a pretty penny, I dare say. *(picking up the plaster nose he's been fashioning)* Hey, look at that. Not too big, not too small. A perfect saintly snout. *(fitting the nose onto the frieze)* Poor fellah. Hardly dignified to have your nose lopped off. Now he'll smell as well as you or I. What do you think?

THOMAS I think it suits him.

PLASTERER Doesn't it. It is a proud nose. Dignified. A well proportioned snoot. No one wants a saint with a great hooky beak, now do they.

THOMAS *has picked up the bucket of plaster.*

Hey, don't touch it! It sticks like sins to the devil.

THOMAS What's in it?

PLASTERER Lime and gypsum, same as most folks use – and then... something special.

THOMAS What's that?

PLASTERER Malt.

THOMAS Malt?

PLASTERER Yes. Malt, like what's in beer. Who'd have thought of them saints being stuck together with ale. It don't half work though, that nose ain't going nowhere.

THOMAS You're a good man. To see this place restored.

PLASTERER It pays my way. And if it helps me to heaven then all the better.

THOMAS Tell me. I had a friend. A Priest. I hoped he might have returned.

PLASTERER They're all new clergy here. I wouldn't know.

A lady, **MRS PREST***, has arrived and stands nearby.*

PLASTERER *(noticing her)* The Priest is busy, ma'am. He's still in prayer.

MRS PREST I only come for God.

PLASTERER He's busy too. He's talking to the Priest.

MRS PREST *moves over to look at the plaster he's using.*

MRS PREST Why restore them when in days they'll lose their heads?

PLASTERER I just do what I'm told. As good Queen **MARY** would have me do –

MRS PREST *(to herself)* The Catholic whore.

PLASTERER Hey, don't go touching that!

MRS PREST *(picking up a pot of sand and casting it down)* You will be damned!

THOMAS Madam!

PLASTERER She's mad.

MRS PREST This is the devil's work.

THOMAS Restrain yourself. You're in a house of God.

MRS PREST You will be / cursed!

She takes a flame…

THOMAS Wait –

MRS PREST You and these idols too.

THOMAS I beg / you –

PLASTERER Put it / down. Stop her!

*Too late – she has set fire to a crucifix. The two men try and wrestle her to the ground. She puts up an angry fight. The following dialogue underscores the fight. Perhaps music plays (*Why Fumeth*).*

MRS PREST You sinners! How can you stand in a house of God and hold up a whore in his place? This is His house. His bequest and you spit upon his name.

PLASTERER She is the devil.

MRS PREST There's nothing wrong with me. "O God, father of Heaven, have mercy upon the miserable sinners. Spare us, spare us all from the crafts and assaults of the devil, from thy wrath and everlasting damnation. From all the deceits of the world, the flesh, and the devil. From lightnings and tempests, from plague and pestilence, from vain glory and idolatry – Good Lord, deliver us!"

PLASTERER You whore – you... hold her – / you don't know what you do – you are the devil! The devil!

THOMAS She is possessed – keep back.

MRS PREST You will be damned! / You deny him – he sees you and what you do. Take your hands off me! You are spawn on the devil.

PLASTERER Lay off her. Hold her!

Stop! Enough!

The **PLASTERER** *moves off her. She is bruised and bloodied.* **THOMAS** *stands back.*

THOMAS Enough.

She is down but she is like a wild animal. Her energy is still virulent.

What would your husband say?

MRS PREST I left my husband. And my son. What do you say to that?

PLASTERER She is the devil.

MRS PREST *spits at him. He is about to launch at her and* **THOMAS** *puts his hand out to stop him.*

THOMAS Stand back. She is possessed.

MRS PREST I know my own mind. I am an honest woman, Sir.

THOMAS You left your spouse!

MRS PREST He loved the Popish whore.

THOMAS There are listeners everywhere – if they hear you.

MRS PREST This charnel house will fall –

THOMAS Do you not hear me?!

PLASTERER She has Lucifer in her.

THOMAS You will be burnt!

MRS PREST You think I'm scared of death?

PLASTERER She has no soul – she is a witch.

MRS PREST I am no witch. But because I am a woman you think me weak. I love my God, Sir. You think I need a mortal man to love? To break myself in twain to give him heirs? You think my soul cannot endure? God sees not my sex.

THOMAS Madam –

MRS PREST *(to the* **PRIEST***)* Let me tell you, Sir, I have but one husband, who stands by me in this room, who will stand by me always and from whom I'll not depart. And that is Jesus Christ.

THOMAS You have a child?

MRS PREST I do.

THOMAS Then for his sake –

MRS PREST I'd rather take him with me to the grave than hear him speak a word of Popish sin.

THOMAS Then they will send you to your death. And may God forgive you for your sins.

MRS PREST Damn you. Damn you and all your saints to the devil! *(exits)*

THOMAS She will be killed.

PLASTERER And so she ought.

A beat. **THOMAS** *looks at him. The* **PLASTERER** *is broken.*

That's fourteen days of labour charred to soot. I have three babes. And now we will not eat. The devil take her soul.

Music might play (e.g. If Ye Love Me*).*

Scene Six
Dr Dee

MARY 1 *is on the throne.* **ELIZABETH** *waits in the wings.*

In a house in Mortlake, **DR DEE,** *the Magus, is channeling the spirit of the Archangel Gabriel. Odd sounds reverberate around the room; a spirit soundscape. A round black mirror hangs on a stand, through which he believes the spirit has arrived. As* **DR DEE** *speaks, a young* **ELIZABETH** *arrives and watches him. He doesn't acknowledge her presence.*

DEE I am Prince of the Seas.

My power is upon the water.

I drowned Pharaoh.

My name was known to Moses.

ELIZABETH Dr Dee?

DEE *holds up his hand in her direction to indicate not to interrupt.*

DEE I am climbing Jacob's ladder.

ELIZABETH Who are you talking to?

DEE Gabriel.

ELIZABETH The angel Gabriel?

DEE He is here.

ELIZABETH Can you see him?

DEE He is behind you.

She goes to turn round.

Don't look! He is flighty. Speak to him, if you wish.

ELIZABETH How might one speak to an angel?

DEE As you would to me. You mustn't fear him.

ELIZABETH Lord, Angel Gabriel, bless me and forgive my sins. *(pause)* What's happening?

DEE He is thinking. You are greatly blessed.

ELIZABETH He said that? May I ask him a question?

DEE Go ahead.

ELIZABETH Tell me, oh spirit, am I to be Queen? *(pause)* Why does he not speak?

DEE Madam, listen.

The spooky sound gets louder.

Look to the obsidian. He moves towards it. He will pass through.

The strange sound ripples round the space as if Gabriel is passing through into the other world. Simultaneously, a number of candles go out, as if by magic. **ELIZABETH** *is overwhelmed.*

ELIZABETH Why did he go? He did not like my question. He was afraid to say.

DEE He is an Angel, he does not feel. No Madam, he had answered you already.

ELIZABETH And?

DEE There is no doubt. You will be Queen.

ELIZABETH Do not speak so unless you're sure.

DEE It is written. Look to the stone.

ELIZABETH I've heard tell of it. It is from the New World. Is it safe?

DEE Of course.

ELIZABETH *(touching it and looking at it closely)* I find nothing in it but patterns in the rock.

DEE Most see nothing at all. You must be truly blessed, for the patterns you see here are etched by God. All of life is written in numbers, Elizabeth. It is divine mathematics, and when one learns how to calculate, one may read what is to come. You will be Queen.

ELIZABETH You are certain?

DEE Yes, but there are forces from Lucifer that your needs must face with strength. It will not be easy. But your countrymen will stand behind you.

ELIZABETH I wouldn't have believed you, but it seems the tides have turned that way. Yesterday, as I rowed out in the Thames, people came to watch me sailing past. Boats drew alongside. A few at first, then more and more until there were a hundred rowers about me, with trumpets, drums and flutes and guns and squibs. And they called my name. Women threw me eglantine and garlands of sarsenet, minstrels played and the children ran along the banks onto the bridge. And all the time they called my name. Elizabeth, Elizabeth for Queen. I think they love me, Doctor. But if Mary's baby is a boy –

DEE There will be no heir.

ELIZABETH But she is with child.

DEE Her belly's swelled, indeed. But it is only a spirit child. Her womb is hollow.

ELIZABETH It cannot be.

DEE She will never make an heir. The mantle is yours. Progress is hatched and like a fire will not be stopped.

ELIZABETH Then you must find me an auspicious day, when all the forces of the heavens align. That day will I be crowned.

DEE Of course. Do you fear it?

ELIZABETH No. But I despise the rocks that have to fall to clear the way. What will become of my sister? For whilst she's given me every cause for hate, she is my kin and I do love her.

DEE Her fate is cast. There is no other way.

ELIZABETH Surely you can change the tides? If you know what is to come –

DEE It has been written in the sand since Jacob's time. And what's written cannot be undone.

ELIZABETH Why can't the hand of rule pass gently from soul to soul? Why death? Why such grief? When my mother died I remember the crowds. People cheered for her head. They cheered.

DEE You must keep faith. There is a fire in you, with which same flame God sent Moses his sign. It is an ancient fire – and marks you out. And you will use it for good, to light the way. But...

ELIZABETH But I must burn the trees that block in my path. The very physic of our land must change. The people are tired, they have been blown from port to port. The church is at sea. I will make change.

DEE You will bring peace to the church.

ELIZABETH You sound certain.

DEE We're entering the seventh age, and seven being unequal, forecasts change. The first age was in the days of Enoch, the second in Noah's time, the third in the days of Moses, the fourth under the King of Israel and the fifth at Christ's Incarnation, when the Roman Empire was at the highest. The days of Charles the Great brought in the sixth, which leads us here – to the seventh, and the last. And like the Sabbath, it brings a time of rest.

ELIZABETH The Ancient scholars prophecised as much. Before the universe should be destroyed, there would be a quiet age, wherein Religion and politick government should agree and conform to the will of God. I never thought that I should lead that charge.

DEE And in your new church let there be simple love of God. Let them pray, and bring them music.

ELIZABETH Music?

DEE Only in song do we come close to the sacred state of heaven. Octaves are divinely numbered threads. Instruct your men to honour them. You have a man, whose music I have heard, who under King Henry wrote such songs.

ELIZABETH Thomas Tallis.

DEE Tell him to set his melody in celestial forms. There must be harmony. Polyphony. He must write the sound of Angels. It is the surest way to God.

ELIZABETH Not for my people. They are simple. They cannot understand the sacred sounds. He will write for them in tones they understand.

DEE But Madam –

ELIZABETH There will be polyphony, but only in my chapel. For me he will write tones unheard by mortal ear before. You say that I am blessed, the Angels spoke as much.

DEE You have my word.

ELIZABETH Invoke them here again. If I'm to bear this mantle I will speak to them myself.

Scene Seven
Doubt

In ELIZABETH*'s early reign.*

TALLIS *is rehearsing his choir (perhaps singing* Nunc Dimittis from the Magnificat*). Mid song* TALLIS *attempts to stops them.*

TALLIS *(quietly)* Enough.

The choir sing on.

(loudly) Enough!

The choir fall silent. TALLIS *says nothing. He is wrestling with a thought.*

A SINGER Sir?

TALLIS It is not right. It's not... *(pause. He gathers himself)* As you were. From *Lumen*

The choir continue to sing.

Silence!

The choir stop mid line.

I cannot bear it. I hate it.

SINGER 2 But Sir, it's glorious.

TALLIS It is. It is divine. And that is why I cannot bear to hear it...

He walks away. The SINGERS *wait.*

These notes. Every line that I have set. Every sound, every rest, a lifetime's study. Night upon night in freezing chancels, fingers numbed, candles burnt to the wax. And for what? For her? Alone? I write for God.

Beyond these walls, the country's doused in blood. It is in the air. In my throat. It chokes me. And yet here. Look. *(he takes in the Royal chapel)* Oh glorious! All gold. Abundance. Majesty. What artistry, what charms for her delight, when outside her people writhe in bile and blood. It is not right. I will not...

He stands. Lost for a moment.

Listen.

Now there is no sound.

No song, no prayer, only the hush of...

He witnesses the silence.

Say nothing of this. Not a word. You hear?

The choir acknowledge him and leave. TALLIS *is left alone.*

What land is this where for one soul's quiet faith

A fellow man can rob him of his life?

And whilst he falls, what of me?

I write a melody.

How will I stand, when judged in front of God?

Is any calling worth such sacrifice?

I will not write for her.

I write for God.

Father, who art in heaven

Wash these notes clean of my blood.

Music swells. Perhaps Let God Arise in Majesty.

Scene Eight
Incarceration

In **ELIZABETH***'s late reign.*

In a cell, the **PRIEST** *is alone, praying in silence. A woman,* **MARY,** *arrives. She carries a bowl of water and a cloth. She watches him, then puts her bowl down and places her hand gently on his shoulder.*

MARY Don't be scared.

PRIEST *(reeling away)* What are you doing!

MARY I didn't mean to startle you. I've brought you water to wash.

PRIEST You've come to take me?

MARY No. Just to visit.

PRIEST Visit?

MARY People tend to like the company.

PRIEST But I am a traitor.

MARY You've never wronged me. Have they fed you?

PRIEST I cannot eat.

MARY I brought you this in case. It's ripe.

She offers him a pear. He takes it and smells it. He stands in thought.

You don't want it?

PRIEST I lived for a time at a place where pears grew. The crop was always good.

MARY It's loam in the soil. It warms the roots, they grow like they've been blessed. Was it holy ground?

PRIEST Yes, it was.

MARY They sometimes call it Juno's fruit. And Aphrodite's. The goddesses all claimed it for their own. It is a comice pear, they have the sweetest taste.

PRIEST Thank you.

MARY Do you miss that place?

PRIEST Sometimes. I had a friend there, who wrote songs like the soul of angels.

MARY What did he play?

PRIEST He sang. And played the organ. I miss that. I'd sit on the stone beam of my window and listen. I often think of that.

MARY Here you can sometimes hear the bells of St Michaels. The music seems to travel on the wind. I find it soothing.

PRIEST It's funny how in sound one can find peace. Music and silence. They are salves to our souls.

MARY What could you see from your window?

PRIEST The tops of cherry trees in the spring. Their blossom strew the paths like snow.

MARY And in the summer?

PRIEST Warblers, when it was warm. They'd fly up the valley and make their nest of moss and bits of wool. Sometimes they'd sing with us at evensong.

The **PRIEST** *winces.*

MARY You are in pain.

PRIEST I can bear it.

MARY Let me help you.

He shies away.

PRIEST This is no place for a woman.

MARY I choose to come.

PRIEST Your husband cannot like it.

MARY He's an understanding man. Besides, I am alone all day. He works 'til there's no light.

PRIEST What is his work?

MARY He works with wood.

PRIEST It is a worthy profession.

MARY It's not your job that makes you good.

PRIEST *(pause)* No. I suppose not.

MARY He has whittled hands. How did they find you?

PRIEST A lady took me in. She cared for me and kept me in the warm. I prayed with her and helped her as I could. Then, one day at dawn she said her friend was ill. The dear man was plagued, a man that once she loved, and would I come with greatest haste, to bless him. I risked the plague to pray with him. Because I wished the poor man to be saved.

And yet he was not sick. Six men were waiting for us at his gate. And as they bound my wrists, she looked away. She couldn't bear to look me in the eye. How is it right that they should both walk free, when I'm to die for my quiet beliefs? I have not sinned. I have not lied. I've killed no man.

*The **PRIEST** winces again.*

MARY Let me tend to you.

*The **PRIEST** is reluctant.*

You cannot offend me. I have been here often. My eyes are accustomed. Please.

He walks downstage to remove his robe. She watches. He takes it off, standing in a loin cloth. He turns up to her and as he does we see his back. It is a tapestry of lash marks. He holds his arms out. He has been flayed on his chest too.

PRIEST Have you seen this before?

She looks at him sadly.

MARY Yes, Sir. Many times. Kneel down. Go on.

He kneels. She takes the bowl and sits next to him. A choir sing in the distance.

You must not fear. Greater is He that is in us, than He that is in the world. The pain you will suffer is short, but your joy will be eternal.

He looks at her. A moment. Then she begins to wash his scars. It hurts him, though she washes gently, a sacred act. As she rings out the cloth the water in the bowl turns red. Some of his lashes are fresh.

As the song ends MARY *leaves with the water and a* GUARD *arrives through a different door. The* PRIEST *remains bent over. He doesn't know she has gone.*

GUARD Sir. It is time. I must ask you once again, do you recant?

PRIEST I cannot.

GUARD Then you will burn.

PRIEST God forgive us both.

GUARD Please stand up.

As the PRIEST *speaks the* GUARD *binds his hands.*

PRIEST Oh Sir, what are we come to? There was a time when my faith meant life. And you by yours may have been condemned. I thought this was to be a time of peace. But fear has never died.

GUARD If you will not recant, then I must take you.

PRIEST Then we will go.

GUARD Sir, by the orders of the crown, you will be transported to Tyburn. There your feet and hands will be bound and a rope placed around your neck. You will be chained to the stake and piled about with coals, which will be lit about you. The rope around your neck will be pulled tight and the fire will engulf you. You will burn unto a powder. *(pause)* You will not recant?

PRIEST I will not.

The **GUARD** *hesitates.*

GUARD Sir, I pray – will you forgive me, for I am not guilty of your death.

PRIEST Come hither.

The **GUARD** *steps towards him. The* **PRIEST** *kisses him on the cheek.*

I forgive you with all my heart.

GUARD Now, if you are ready then you must follow me.

PRIEST But what of the woman? Don't lock her in behind me.

GUARD What woman, Sir?

PRIEST The visitor. She washed my wounds and prayed with me.

GUARD Your cell was locked. There was no woman, Sir.

The **PRIEST** *takes this in. He walks out accompanied by the* **GUARD**. *Music begins. Perhaps* Jesu Salvator Seculae. **THOMAS TALLIS** *arrives to witness the magnificence of the music.*

Finis

Property List

Candle (p1)

Glass of wine (p6)

Chalice of wine (p6)

Incense (p8)

Crosses (p8)

Candelabras (p8)

Bible (p8)

The church is dismantled piece by piece, candles are snuffed out, until the stage is left bare, except a table (p12)

Pear (p13)

Knife (p13)

Manuscript (p13)

Scroll (p14)

He has a box of wares, covered in horse skin. It is knocked about, as is he (p18)

Candle (p19)

Lace (p19)

Beads (p19)

Slate (p19)

A chalice (p19)

The PLASTERER, sits making a paste. He is restoring the figures in a Catholic frieze in which the saints have been damaged (22)

Books (p22)

Plaster nose (p22)

Pot of sand (p24)

Flame (candle) (p24)

She has set fire to a crucifix (p24)

A round black mirror hangs on a stand (p28)

Bowl of water (p35)

Cloth (p35)

Pear (p35)

As she rings out the cloth the water in the bowl turns red (p38)

Guard binds his hands (p38)

Lighting

Simultaneously, a number of candles go out, as if by magic (p29)

Sound/Music Notes

Ideally, the play would be staged with a choir performing the music, but it could also be staged with recorded music.

A single voice sings an undecorated Amen. Then a more ornate Allelujah (p2)

We hear a choir sing (perhaps *Videte Miraculum*). It is glorious. (p2)

A solo musician might play for his entertainment (p3)

The singer sings a Tallis song (perhaps *Like a Doleful Dove*) (p7)

Perhaps we hear music (Tallis' *E'en like the Hunted*) (p7)

Choral music plays (perhaps Tallis' *Videte Miraculum*) It is glorious, big, Catholic. (p8)

Perhaps music plays (e.g. *O Nata Lux*) p12)

He tries singing a line.

(sung) *God grant us grace.*

Then as he writes, we hear it sung. He makes changes as he goes, scribbling, stopping, starting. He is struggling. English is not as beautiful as Latin. We listen to *Gaude Gloriosa* (p12)

The song continues (p13)

A nightingale sings (p17)

We hear a piece of music in which a single voice is joined by another and another until the whole choir are singing (for example *God Grant Us Grace*). The result is magnificent in its simplicity (p17)

Perhaps music plays (*Why Fumeth*) (p24)

Music might play (e.g. *If Ye Love Me*) (p27)

Odd sounds reverberate around the room; a spirit soundscape (p28)

The spooky sound gets louder (p29)

The strange sound ripples round the space as if Gabriel is passing through into the other world (p29)

Tallis is rehearsing his choir (perhaps singing *Nunc Dimittis from the Magnificat*) (p33)

Music swells. Perhaps *Let God Arise in Majesty* (p33)

Music begins. Perhaps *Jesu Salvator Seculae* (p40)

Costume:

HENRY VIII is seated in his boudoir in night attire – a white billowing robe (p3)

A PEDDLER enters. He is the priest from Waltham Abbey, now disguised (p18)

PRIEST - He walks downstage to remove his robe. She watches. He takes it off, standing in a loin cloth. He turns up to her and as he does we see his back. It is a tapestry of lash marks. He holds his arms out. He has been flayed on his chest too (p38)

Lightning Source UK Ltd.
Milton Keynes UK
UKOW06f2301191015

260967UK00001B/1/P